Better Slam Bidding with Bergen

By Marty Bergen

Bergen Books

Bergen Books
9 River Chase Terrace
Palm Beach Gardens, FL 33418-6817

First Edition published 2008.
Printed in the United States of America.
10 9 8 7 6 5 4 3 2 1

First Printing: October 2008

Library of Congress Control Number: 2008908950

ISBN: 0-9744714-8-8

Marty's New Website:

www.martybergen.com

Special features that can benefit YOU:

- Partnership slam checklists: print all you need
- Partnership bidding – with answers and explanations
- Tips from Marty
- Links to free sites to practice on
- Marty's class notes
- Links to worthwhile bridge sites
- Highlights from Marty's books
- Special offers on Marty's books and CDs
- Free demo chapters of Marty's two CDs
- Bidding quizzes – with answers and explanations
- Updates on upcoming seminars and cruises
- One-on-one (or group) lessons with Marty
- Books and CDs by other authors

My Very Special Thanks to:

Editors and Writers: Allison Brandt and Mike Giesler.
Your effort, expertise, and eagle eyes have made all the difference.

Printer: Karl Frauhammer. Definitely a mensch.

Larry Cohen, Richard Oshlag, Carl Ritner:
When I needed help, they were always there.

Thanks To:

Cheryl Angel, Heidi Atkinson, Margaret and Ted Baldwin,
Jorge Barrera, Cheryl Bergen, Trish and John Block, Lori Block,
Richard Brandenburg, Linda Burke, Ollie Burno, Jim Canty,
Felice Carpenter, Bill Collis, Nancy Conway, Pearl Cooper,
Marti Cowie, Nancy Deal, Teri Dolci, Mitch Edelman, Ed Evers,
Pete Filandro, Howard Friedel, William Frisby, Jim Garnher,
Terry Gerber, Steve Gerhard, Lyn Giuffrida, Pat and Gordon Gray,
Shana Green, Peter Halmos, Wendi Halvorsen, Tish Hamblin,
Lorraine Hanna, Pat Harrington, Marilyn and Malcom Jones,
Steve Jones, Herbert Jordan, Eddie Kantar, Carol Kaplan,
Doris Katz, Al Kimel, Danny Kleinman, Dee Korenbaum, Gail
Kreppel, Alan Lipner, Harriet and Dave Morris, Julie Murphy,
Sally Nathanson, Elizabeth Nelson, Phyllis Nicholson,
Mary Oshlag, Barry Patten, Carl Perchonock, Helene Pittler,
Ricardo Poleschi, David Pollard, Ellen Caitlin Pomer, David Porter,
Margie Quinto, Jesse Reisman, Mark Rosenholz, Pete Rudie,
John Rudy, Shag Sameach, Eric Sandberg, Arthur Schein,
Judy and Jim Schorner, Howard Schutzman, Ellie Schwartz,
Eliot Sepinuck, Peggy Shuping, Maggie Sparrow, Everne Spiegel,
Claire Stern, Merle Stetser, Bobby Stinebaugh, Jim Stokes,
Sandy Strine, Henry Sun, Kristofor Varhus, Bob Varty,
Mym Young, and Jeanne Zach.

Typesetting, layout, and editing by
Hammond Graphics

CONTENTS

More Good Stuff

Chapter 1
How To Improve
Your Slam Bidding

For a bridge player, I can't imagine anything more exciting than bidding and making a slam. Although slam bidding is difficult, I believe that, regardless of your level, every player and every partnership can take steps to greatly improve their bidding.

Here are my recommendations:

1. Every partnership needs a bridge notebook.
You must have your agreements in writing. I suggest getting started by creating a folder on your computer or by using a notebook if you prefer pen and paper. A well-organized table of contents is a must. Each section should include all of your agreements, as well as, the relevant conventions. Here are my suggestions for sections in a notebook on slam bidding:

- Conventions dealing with aces (and keycards).
- After we open one of a major.
- After we open one of a minor.
- After our notrump opening bids.
- After we open 2♣.
- Other slam conventions.
- Control-bidding.
- After an opponent preempts.
- Other competitive auctions.
- Philosophy and bidding style for each partner, such as how aggressive he is, etc.

2. Playing is not enough. Many players believe that the key to bidding better is playing often. That is not true. If your only contact with the game is playing, the most likely result is that you are repeating errors and reinforcing misconceptions. I am certainly not suggesting that you stop playing, but if you are serious about bidding better, you must be willing to do more.

3. Each player must improve his bidding skills. What topic should you begin with? That's easy. Without question – it's hand evaluation. In fact, every player interested in improving his bidding must begin there. It is the key to good bidding, and the area where players can most easily improve. All that is needed is a player who is open-minded enough to learn a sensible method of correctly evaluating hands. Two good places to start are *Slam Bidding Made Easier* and this book. Of course, you must always remember that bridge books should be studied – as opposed to reading casually and hoping for magic through osmosis.

Obviously, learning from a knowledgeable teacher or friend is also an option. Thanks to the Internet, there are numerous opportunities to learn online as well. Several recommended websites are listed on page 64.

4. Improving the Partnership
In addition to the bidding notebook, there are many other ways to enable you and your partner to bid more effectively than you ever have.

A. Discussing and filling out the checklists in this workbook is a good place to start. I'd also suggest recording all new agreements in your notebook.

B. I urge partnerships to discuss bridge and bridge auctions in a constructive way. For example, after a Jacoby 2NT response, what does opener's jump in a new suit show? You really should discuss:

- How good does the side suit have to be?
- Does the bid say anything about opener's HCP?
- Is a side-suit void possible?
- Do we like this bid, or prefer showing a short suit?

You might say, "But Marty, we'd never think of all that. We're not experts." That's what the checklists are all about. You don't have to come up with the various possibilities – they're already laid out for you.

C. I strongly recommend bidding hands together. You'll be amazed how much you can learn during a 30-minute practice session with your partner. When experts prepare for a tournament, they don't rush out to play bridge; instead, they bid hands.

Computer-savvy readers can easily generate hands for slam bidding or any other topic. Some books have hands to bid (see page 63 for a good one). There are also Internet sites that include practice hands. I will include some on my website (page 3).

However, some players prefer bidding with cards. I use a method that works very well for both students and experts. I'll describe it on the next page.

Easy, Fun, and Very Beneficial for Slam Bidding

When I suggest to my students that they practice bidding with their partner, many of them tell me that they relate much better to actual cards than to hands on paper. Here's an easy method to practice with a deck of cards. It is designed for slam bidding for two players, but in a pinch, you can even do it on your own.

• Remove six small clubs and seven small diamonds and put them aside. If you are more interested in practicing minor-suit slam bidding, remove hearts and spades instead.

• Deal the 39 remaining cards face down into three piles. Each partner picks up a hand. If a player gets a weak hand, he exchanges his cards for the third hand.

• The dealer bids first, and partner responds. Each player records the auction. The opponents never bid. The bidding continues until someone passes.

• When the auction is over, look at each other's hands and constructively discuss the bidding. Take notes regarding agreements and tendencies, and put them into your bridge notebook.

• Shuffle and redeal the "good" 39 cards, vary the dealer, and repeat the exercise as often as you like.

In conclusion, I hope that some/all of the suggestions in this chapter help you become a better slam bidder, and therefore, a better bridge player.

Chapter 2
Hand Evaluation

Good hand evaluation is essential to successful slam bidding – you can't bid well without it. Conventions can be helpful, but they are NOT the key to good bidding. It's fun to be dealt a lot of good cards, but that alone doesn't guarantee anything. In the long run, what you need to bid well is good judgment, and the secret to good judgment is good hand evaluation.

For effective hand evaluation, you *must not* be a slave to your HCP. You need to examine a hand from different perspectives and upgrade or downgrade depending on several factors.

Might making these upgrades and downgrades seem like too much work? To some, it will. But, before you decide to skip this chapter and get to the conventions, I'd like to ask you a question or two.

What would be your first thought if you encountered a pair at a Regional and read "Frequent upgrades and some downgrades" at the top of their convention card? Would you think that they were aspiring players who had just read a bridge book and were eager to apply their newly-acquired knowledge? That would certainly be an understandable reaction.

"Marty, you made this up so we'll read this chapter. I've been playing forever and I've never seen anything like that. Only a pair of country bumpkins would have that statement on their card."

For your information, I did not make it up. And I believe that referring to these players as "a pair of country bumpkins" is not really fair. Actually, they have done rather well for themselves. You might even have heard of them. Their names are Jeff Meckstroth and Eric Rodwell (aka Meckwell). I would mention their number of National and World Championships, but they win so often that the number has probably changed since this book went to print!

What's my point? If the best pair in the world believes that upgrading and downgrading is necessary and important for them, then the possibility exists that it might also prove to be beneficial for YOU.

This chapter will provide a summary of the evaluation techniques that I described in *Slam Bidding Made Easier* (SBME). For effective hand evaluation, you *must* look beyond your HCP and know how to:

☑ Evaluate your hand before the auction begins;

☑ Make the correct adjustments for distribution;

☑ Correctly re-evaluate when you find a fit.

Of course, for those readers who can already evaluate as well as Jeff and Eric, I agree that *you* don't need to review how to figure out what your hand is really worth. However, for those players who aren't sure that their evaluation skills compare favorably with Jeff and Eric, you probably should read on.

Starting Points

As soon as you pick up your cards, you should count your *starting points* – which represents the true value of your hand before the auction. Once you do this for a few hands, the process will become as easy as pie.

A. Adjust-3 (to ensure HCP accuracy)

Step 1:   Count underrated honors: (aces + tens).
Step 2:   Count overrated quacks (queens + jacks).
           (Note: no adjustment is needed for kings.)
Step 3:   Subtract the smaller number from the larger.
Step 4:   Consider the difference:
           If 0-2, no adjustment is needed.
           If 3-5, adjust by 1 point.
           If 6+ (rare), adjust by 2 points.
Step 5:   If you have more underrated honors, add.
           If you have more overrated honors, subtract.

B. Dubious Doubletons and Singletons
Subtract 1 point for each of these holdings.
Doubleton: KQ, KJ, QJ, Qx, Jx
Singleton: K, Q, or J

C. Quality Suits
A suit with 3+ honors and 4+ cards.
Add one point for each quality suit.

D. Length
Add for *long* suits:
    1 point for each 5-card suit;
    2 points for each 6-card suit;
    3 points for a 7-card suit, etc.

Counting *starting points:*

1. Add up your HCP.

2. Apply Adjust-3 in case the # of HCP needs adjusting.

3. Subtract 1 point each if any dubious short suits.
   The result of steps 1-3 is your adjusted HCP.

4. Add 1 point each if any quality suits.

5. Add length points if any 5+ card suits.

The result of steps 1-5 is your *starting points.*

Example 1: ♠ A 10 7 3 2   ♡ A K 10 8   ◇ J 2   ♣ 8 2

12 HCP:

Adjust-3: 4 upgrades (2 aces, 2 tens),
1 downgrade (jack).
4 – 1 = 3, so add one point.   12 HCP + 1 = 13

Dubious Short Suits: Subtract for the ◇J 2.   −1

Quality Suits: Add for the quality heart suit.   +1

Length: Add for the 5-card spade suit.   +1

starting points: 14

Example 2: ♠ 9   ♡ A Q J 7 5 4   ◇ A K J 3   ♣ 7 5

15 HCP

Adjust-3: 2 upgrades (aces),
3 downgrades (1 queen, 2 jacks).
3 – 2 = only 1, so no adjustment.
HCP: 15

Quality Suits: Add for the 2 quality suits.   +2

Length: Add for the 6-card suit.   +2

starting points: 19

Conclusion: Example 2 is a very upgradable hand.

Re-evaluating by Dummy After a Fit

When you have support for partner's major suit, you expect to be the dummy. If you have a short suit (or two), here is the correct way to add points:

Counting Dummy's Short-Suit Points

Doubleton = 1 point for each one.
Singleton = 2 points, but 3 points with 4+ trumps.
Void = # trumps in dummy's hand. Dummy should NOT count 5 points for a void unless he has 5 trumps.

To know how many dummy points you have, add your short-suit points to your *starting points*.
That's all you need to do.

Answer these questions for hands 1- 4.
A. How many *starting points* do you have?
B. How many dummy points do you have?
C. What's your bid?

You	Partner
1♢	1♠
???	

1.   ♠ A K 10 2   ♡ 8 5   ♢ A K 10 9   ♣ 7 6 4
14 HCP
Adjust-3: Add 1 point (4 upgrades, no downgrades).
Quality Suits: Add 2 points (2 quality suits).
17 *starting points* (14 + 1 + 2 = 17).
Short Suits: Add 1 point (doubleton).
Total: 18 dummy points.
Bid 3♠ with this *very* upgradable hand.

2. ♠ K 6 5 4 ♡ A 7 4 2 ◇ K J 7 6 ♣ Q
13 HCP
Adjust-3: No adjustment (1 upgrade, 2 downgrades).
Dubious Short Suits: Subtract 1 point (♣Q).
Length: None.
12 starting points (13 − 1 = 12).
Short Suits: Add 3 points (singleton with 4 trumps).
Total: 15 dummy points.
Raise to 2♠.

3. ♠ A J 9 ♡ A 8 6 4 ◇ K 10 7 5 3 ♣ J
13 HCP
Adjust-3: No adjustment (3 upgrades, 2 downgrades).
Dubious Short Suits: Subtract 1 point (♣J).
Length: Add 1 point (5-card diamond suit).
13 starting points (13 − 1 + 1 = 13).
Short Suits: Add 2 points (singleton with 3 trumps).
Total: 15 dummy points.
Raise to 2♠.

4. ♠ A 9 7 3 ♡ — ◇ A Q 10 6 3 ♣ A 10 7 6
14 HCP
Adjust-3: Add 1 point (5 upgrades, 1 downgrade).
Quality Suits: Add 1 point for the nice diamond suit.
Length: Add 1 point (5-card diamond suit).
17 starting points (14 + 1 + 1 + 1 = 17).
Short Suits: Add 4 points (void with 4 trumps).
Total: 21 dummy points.
Bid 4♡ (splinter). If not playing splinters, bid 4♠.

Re-evaluating by Declarer After a Fit

When partner raises your major suit, you expect to be the declarer. You can then re-evaluate your hand for "Bergen Points." Here's a review of the techniques that you should use:

1. **Begin with your number of *starting points.***

2. **Short Suits:**
   Singleton: Add 2 points.
   Void: Add 4 points.
   One doubleton: Do not add anything.
   2-3 doubletons: Add exactly 1 point.

3. **Long Trumps:**
   Add 1 point for each trump after five.
   Therefore, you should add:
   1 point for a 6-card suit;
   2 points for a 7-card suit;
   3 points for an 8-card suit.

4. **Side Suits:**
   Add 1 point for a suit with 4+ cards.

Total Points
Once you apply steps 1-4 to re-evaluate, the total is your *Bergen Points.* Then, add your Bergen Points to the number of points partner promised. That will tell you whether your side has the 33 *total points* needed for a possible slam. If your total points are less than 33, forget about slam.

Each of the following hands have 18 *starting points.*
If you get lucky and partner supports your spades,
how many Bergen Points will you have?

1. ♠ A J 8 5 4 3   ♡ A Q 5 2   ◇ —   ♣ K Q 3
Short Suits: Add 4 points (void).
Long Trumps: Add 1 point (6 trumps).
Side Suits: Add 1 point (4-card heart suit).
Total: 24 Bergen Points (18 + 4 + 1 + 1 = 24).

2. ♠ A K 9 7 3   ♡ K 8   ◇ 6 4   ♣ A Q 10 3
Short Suits: Add 1 point (for the 2 doubletons).
Side Suits: Add 1 point (4-card club suit).
Total: 20 Bergen Points (18 + 1 + 1 = 20).

3. ♠ Q J 8 7 3   ♡ A Q 9 5 2   ◇ K 9   ♣ A
Short Suits: Add 2 points (singleton).
Side Suits: Add 1 point (5-card heart suit).
Total: 21 Bergen Points (18 + 2 + 1 = 21).

4. ♠ A K Q 10 7 3   ♡ K 10 2   ◇ 8 6   ♣ K 3
Short Suits: Add 1 point (for the 2 doubletons).
Long Trumps: Add 1 point (6 trumps).
Total: 20 Bergen Points (18 + 1 + 1 = 20).

5. ♠ K J 9 8 7 5 2   ♡ A K J   ◇ K 3   ♣ 8
Short Suits: Add 2 points (singleton).
Long Trumps: Add 2 points (7 trumps).
Total: 22 Bergen Points (18 + 2 + 2 = 22).

Misfits

In both this book and SBME, the focus is on hands where your side has a fit. Because re-evaluating after you've found a fit is so important, that decision was intentional. However, in real life, you don't have a fit on every hand. Therefore, I'll use this page to look at life on the other side of town.

Consider this nice hand:

♠ K J 7 6 4 3   ♡ A Q 7 2   ◇ 7   ♣ A J

15 HCP +2 (6-card suit) = 17 *starting points.*

The auction proceeds:

Partner	You
1◇	1♠
3◇	3♡
3NT	???

Partner has a nice hand with a strong diamond suit. A typical example would include 16 HCP. You not only dislike his diamonds, but he has not shown any interest in your suits either. Everything about this hand indicates that it is a misfit. What would you do?

When the hand is a misfit, count HCP only.
You are no longer entitled to your length points, so the value of this hand should be reduced to 15. After making this adjustment, you should pass 3NT. Slams and misfits are NOT compatible.

Which Points Are Which?

Starting Points:
What? The value of a hand before the auction.
When? Before the auction begins.
Who? A must for both partners.
Technique? Add adjusted HCP* + quality suits
+ length points.

Dummy Points:
What? The value of dummy's hand after a fit.
When? You raise partner's major suit.
Who? The player who expects to be dummy.
Technique? Add *starting points* + short-suit points.

Bergen Points:
What? The value of declarer's hand after a raise.
When? Partner raises your major suit.
Who? The player who expects to be declarer.
Technique? Add *starting points* + short-suit points
+ long-trump points + side-suit points.

Total Points:
What? The sum of Bergen Points + dummy points
(the total # of points for the partnership).
When? Partner's point-count is well-defined.
Who? Declarer, but dummy can apply it at times.
Technique? Add your # of points to partner's #.
Do you have 33? Yes, no, maybe?
If no, forget about slam.

*Adjusted HCP is the result of: HCP, Adjust-3,
and subtracting for dubious short suits.

Chapter 3
Control-Bids

Historically, these have been described as "cue-bids."
Because that term refers to bids in an opponent's suit,
I much prefer thinking of slam tries as "control-bids."
This term was coined by *The Bridge World.*

Although control-bidding will never be as popular with
the masses as Blackwood, it is essential. However, I
believe that: **Any pair that doesn't use control-bids
has no chance to be effective in slam bidding.**
Control-bids allow your side to exchange information
about controls at a low level and still have the ability
to use Blackwood later on.

Important FYI: Control-bids are not a trivial topic.
In my attempt to make it as clear as possible, I will
NOT include two types of auctions in the discussion:

1. Auctions where a minor suit is bid and raised.
Now, a new suit at the three level is usually an attempt
to play in 3NT – rather than a control-bid.

2. Two-Over-One Game-Forcing auctions.
When a major suit has been supported at the two level,
2/1 pairs differ as to which bids at the three level show
distribution and which ones are control-bids.

Therefore, all discussions of control-bids in this book
and in SBME are confined to auctions where a major
suit was agreed by a Jacoby 2NT response or a raise
to the three or four level.

Before discussing control-bidding auctions and the decisions that every partnership must make, I find a Q&A approach to be helpful in getting started.

What is a control?
A holding in a side suit that will usually not result in two quick losers in the suit.
Aces and voids are first-round controls.
Kings and singletons are second-round controls.

What is a control-bid?
A slam try which promises a control in the suit bid. The control is usually an ace or king. Control-bids are always non-jump bids in a side suit.

When is a control-bid made?
After a major suit is agreed in a game-forcing auction.

At what level are control-bids made?
Control-bidding usually begins at the four level.
On certain auctions, a 3-level control-bid is possiible.

It is now time for the partnership to make the crucial control-bidding decision that will greatly affect all of their control-bidding auctions. The question addresses each player's first control-bid of the auction. Does the bid promise a first-round control in the suit, or can you make the bid with either a first-round control or a second-round control? The latter approach is often referred to as "Italian control-bidding."

Do all experts, authors and teachers prefer the same approach? No way! They agree to disagree.
What are my thoughts? Turn the page to find out.

> *You*   *Partner*
> 1♠   4♣
> ???

♠ A K J 10 5 3 ♡ Q 5 ◇ 8 ♣ A J 8 6

After partner's Splinter Bid, a spade slam is likely. However, it would be wrong to bid 4NT without a heart control. If partner has one ace, you won't know what to do. 6♠ is cold opposite a hand such as:

♠ Q 9 7 2 ♡ K 7 6 3 ◇ A Q 9 7 ♣ 2

but a heart lead will defeat your slam if partner has:

♠ Q 7 6 4 ♡ J 9 8 7 ◇ A Q J 4 ♣ K

Instead of bidding 4NT, make a control-bid. If playing Italian style, this is an easy hand. Bid 4◇ and await developments. If partner bids 4♡, you'll be delighted to bid 4NT. If he doesn't, you will KNOW that he lacks a heart control, and you'll forget about slam.

However, if your partnership's first control-bid is reserved for first-round controls, you'd have to bid 5♣ and hope to sort things out at the five level. Yuck.

Anyway, whether or not you believe that Italian control-bidding is the way to go, "Viva Italia" is my motto. I was using this approach long before I knew where it originated, and can't imagine ever doing anything else. As far as I'm concerned, **a control-bid below game promises a control; either first-round or second.**

Readers who insist, "The first control-bids promise first-round controls," might not be happy, but I'm now ready to continue with the joy of Italian control-bids.

All controls are bid up-the-line. Therefore, if a player bypasses a suit, he denies a control in that suit. Those two statements are absolutely crucial. This approach allows us to *know* whether we have controls in all three side suits – which is awesome. Because examples are worth much more than words, it's time for a few hands.

1. *West*	*West*	*East*	*East*
♠ A Q 10 3	1♣	1♠	♠ K J 9 5 4 2
♡ A	3♠	4◇	♡ K 9
◇ K 9 4	4♠	Pass	◇ A Q
♣ Q 7 6 5 2			♣ J 8 4

It's obvious that 6♠ would have been hopeless, but did you understand why West did *not* control-bid 4♡? If not, would you believe that the answer was a bid that *wasn't* made? Isn't bridge a great game?

"Enough with the questions, Marty. How about some answers for a change?" Fair enough.

Control-bids are made up-the-line, so when East bid 4◇, he denied a club control – because he bypassed 4♣. Therefore, West knew that it was time to forget about slam. If he had bid 4♡, he would have been telling East, "Not only do I have a heart control, but I also have the club control you said you were missing."

2. West	West	East	East
♠ A 10 6 5	1◇	1♡	♠ 7 2
♡ A J 9 4	3♡	4♣	♡ K 8 7 6 5 3
◇ K Q J 9	4◇	4NT	◇ A
♣ 2	5♡	6♡	♣ K Q 8 4

This hand illustrates the same principle as in the previous example, but this one has a happy ending. East's 4♣ bid shows slam interest but denies a spade control. If West didn't have a spade control, he would have signed off in 4♡. His 4◇ bid showed two controls (spades and diamonds) in one bid.

Once West showed a spade control, East was happy to bid 4NT. East did NOT have a 12-point hand. Here is a review of how East should evaluate his hand.

Before the auction begins:
12 HCP + 2 (6-card suit) = 14 *starting points.*

Re-evaluate after West raised hearts:
14 + 2 (singleton) + 1 (long trumps) + 1 (4 clubs).
Total = 18 Bergen Points (14 + 2 + 1 + 1 = 18).

3. West	West	East	East
♠ K J 8 6 3 2	1♠	2NT	♠ A Q 10 9
♡ K 8 3	3♣	3♡	♡ A Q 10
◇ Q 5 4	4♠	Pass	◇ J 7
♣ A			♣ K 8 4 2

3♣ showed 0-1 club. The 3♡ bid was an example of a rare control-bid at the three level – but denied a diamond control. Therefore, West signed off in game.

4. *West*	*West*	*East*	*East*
♠ A 10 8 3	1♡	1♠	♠ K Q 7 5 4 2
♡ A K 10 9 6	3♠	4♣	♡ 2
◇ 7	4◇	4NT	◇ 10 6 5
♣ 9 6 3	5♡	6♠	♣ A K J

West had a minimum for his jump raise – in fact, some players would have been content to raise to 2♠. Nevertheless, because East was unlimited, West had the obligation to show his control below the level of game. If West had failed to show his diamond control, East would have stopped in 4♠.

Why didn't East bid 4♡ over 4◇? **If partner has shown a 5+ card side suit, a control-bid in that suit should promise the ace or king.**

5. *West*	*West*	*East*	*East*
♠ A K J 7 6 3	1♠	2NT	♠ Q 8 4 2
♡ —	3♡	4♣	♡ A K 9 3
◇ 10 9 4	4♡	4♠	◇ Q 6
♣ K J 9 2	Pass		♣ A Q 4

The 4♡ bid showed a void. **Once you show a short suit, control-bid that suit only with a void – not a singleton ace.** When West bypassed 4◇, East knew that E-W had no diamond control, so he signed off.

One of the big advantages of Italian control-bids is how much you are able to learn about controls while remaining at the four level. Am I admitting that I don't like the five level? Yes, I am. Do I think Italian is the way to go? Yes, I do. Pasta, anyone?

Of course, on some hands, the five level is inevitable. This is more likely to occur when a player makes a bid that uses up a great deal of bidding space.

6. *West*	*West*	*East*	*East*
♠ J 10 7 5 2	1♠	2NT	♠ A K 6 4 3
♡ A K 9 8 2	4♡	5♣	♡ Q 6 4
◇ A 4	5◇	7♠	◇ 8 7
♣ 2	Pass		♣ A J 10

West's 4♡ bid showed a 5-card heart suit with two of the top three honors. East was delighted to hear that, but without a diamond control, it would have been wrong for him to bid 4NT. West could have had a hand where a diamond lead would have been fatal in 6♠, such as:

♠ Q J 8 7 2   ♡ A K J 4 3   ◇ J 2   ♣ 3

Therefore, East control-bid 5♣. This bid promised a *first-round* control in clubs. Why is that?

Because 4NT is no longer available, a 5-level control-bid shows first-round control in that suit. When West bid 5◇, he promised either the ◇ A or a diamond void. If he had second-round control of diamonds, he would jump to 6♠.

That was all East needed to bid the excellent grand slam. Not surprisingly, at the tournament where this hand was actually played, many pairs only got to six.

Partnership Checklist – Control Bids

Use this checklist to firm up your control-bidding agreements. Check A or B on #1. Check Yes or No on #2-6. I recommend B on #1 and Yes on #2-6. Keep in mind that this checklist does not address:

- Auctions where a minor suit is bid and raised;
- 2/1 Game Forcing auctions.

1. Each player's first control-bid promises:

☐ A a first-round control in the suit

☐ B any control (Italian style)

2. Controls are bid up-the-line, so bypassing a suit denies a control in that suit.

☐ Yes ☐ No

3. As long as slam is possible, always show a control below the game level.

☐ Yes ☐ No

4. If partner has shown a 5+ card suit, a control-bid in his suit shows the ace or king.

☐ Yes ☐ No

5. Once you have shown a short suit, only control-bid that suit with a void.

☐ Yes ☐ No

6. A control-bid at the five level shows first-round control in that suit.

☐ Yes ☐ No

Chapter 4
Jacoby 2NT

Most players agree that Jacoby 2NT is "on" when:

*   Partner opens 1♡ or 1♠;
*   You are an unpassed hand;
*   Your RHO passes.

You and your partner should know what your 2NT response would show if you are a passed hand or if your RHO bids or doubles.

The Jacoby 2NT response:

A. Strength

*   Promises 13+ dummy points;
*   Has no upper limit;
*   Could include fewer than 13 HCP.

Note: In this chapter, the opening bid is always 1♠. The same concepts would also apply if the partnership's fit was in hearts.

I would respond 2NT with these hands:

♠ A K 7 6   ♡ 4 3   ◊ 9 7 6 4 3   ♣ A 7

♠ Q 9 4 2   ♡ A K 2   ◊ A J 9   ♣ 4 3 2

♠ K Q J 5   ♡ A 9 6 5   ◊ J 7 5   ♣ A K

B. Distribution

The 2NT bid:

- Promises 4+ trumps;
- Could include a long, strong side suit;
- Might include a singleton.

Responder should only splinter with 13-16 dummy points, so if he has 17+ dummy points, he should respond 2NT.

I would respond 2NT with these hands:

♠ A 6 5 4   ♡ 2   ◇ A J 8 7 6   ♣ A Q 3

♠ K 8 6 2   ♡ A J 10 9 4   ◇ A Q   ♣ 8 4

Opener's Rebids After a Jacoby 2NT Response

A. 3 of a new suit = singleton or void, any strength. I love this economical bid. I am happy to make the bid as often as possible, including all of the following:

- Hands with a singleton honor;
- Hands with a void;
- Hands with a 5-card side suit, regardless of the strength of the suit or the strength of the hand.

♠ A Q 9 7 5   ♡ K Q 8 6 5   ◇ 8 7 5   ♣ —   Bid 3♣

♠ K 10 7 6 5   ♡ A 6   ◇ 8   ♣ K J 7 6 5   Bid 3◇

♠ J 9 8 7 6 4   ♡ A   ◇ K Q 6   ♣ K Q 4   Bid 3♡

B. 4 of a new suit = strong 5-card side suit.
I don't like this non-economical bid at all, and would
much rather show my short suit at the three level.
Therefore, I would make this bid only with a minimum
opening bid and an excellent second suit.
I suggest that this bid shows:

*   10-13 HCP;

*   A 5-card suit with 2 of the top 3 honors;

*   A hand without a void.

♠ Q 9 7 6 5 3   ♡ 7   ◇ 5   ♣ A K J 9 6   Bid 4♣

♠ K Q J 7 6   ♡ 5   ◇ K Q 10 6 4   ♣ J 3   Bid 4◇

♠ K J 8 6 5   ♡ A Q J 6 4   ◇ 7 5   ♣ 4   Bid 4♡

♠ K 9 7 3 2   ♡ A K 7 6 4   ◇ A 5   ♣ 4   Bid 3♣

C. Rebids that deny a short suit.
Important Note: Too many players are guilty of
thinking that the determining factor for these rebids
is the number of HCP. When you have a fit, that is
NEVER true. After a Jacoby 2NT auction, if opener
lacks a short suit, he will rebid based on his number
of Bergen Points.

1. 4♠ = 12-14 Bergen Points, no short suit, 0-2 aces.
Most hands that bid 4♠ have quacks galore.

♠ Q J 7 6 4   ♡ K Q J   ◇ K J 10   ♣ 8 6   Bid 4♠

♠ A K Q J 8   ♡ Q 8 6   ◇ J 5   ♣ 8 7 5   Bid 4♠

♠ K J 8 5 2   ♡ Q J 8 7   ◇ K Q   ♣ Q 9   Bid 4♠

2. 3NT = 15-17 Bergen Points, no short suit.
Bid 3NT with a medium-strength hand. Too many
players incorrectly rebid 4♠ with these decent
opening bids.

♠ A K Q 7 3   ♡ 6 4   ◇ A J 10   ♣ 6 5 4   Bid 3NT

♠ A J 9 7 5   ♡ A K 10 6   ◇ 8 7   ♣ 6 5   Bid 3NT

♠ 9 8 7 6 4 3   ♡ A 5 4   ◇ A 2   ♣ A 3   Bid 3NT

3. 3♠ = 18+ Bergen Points, no short suit.
This bid shows a hand that is very interested in slam.

♠ A 8 7 5 4   ♡ K Q J   ◇ K 7   ♣ K Q 7   Bid 3♠

♠ Q J 7 5 4   ♡ A 5   ◇ A 2   ♣ A Q 9 8   Bid 3♠

♠ K 8 7 5 4 3   ♡ A Q 2   ◇ A Q   ♣ 6 4   Bid 3♠

Responder's Rebids

After opener's rebid, responder will usually explore
for slam by control-bidding his cheapest control.
His other options are to bid:

- 4 of the agreed trump suit. Based on the principle
  of Fast Arrival, this is his most discouraging action.

- 3 of the agreed major to show slam interest.

- 4NT to ask for aces (or keycards).

Partnership Checklist – Jacoby 2NT
Check Yes or No for each statement.

We play Jacoby 2NT.   ☐ Yes   ☐ No

A Jacoby 2NT response is
only "on" by an unpassed hand.   ☐ Yes   ☐ No

A Jacoby 2NT response is
only "on" when RHO passes.   ☐ Yes   ☐ No

A Jacoby 2NT response promises 13+ dummy points,
with no upper limit on strength.   ☐ Yes   ☐ No

A Jacoby 2NT response promises 4+ trumps.
                                   ☐ Yes   ☐ No

A Jacoby 2NT response denies a singleton, unless the
hand has 17+ dummy points.   ☐ Yes   ☐ No

A Jacoby 2NT response can be made
with a long, strong side suit.   ☐ Yes   ☐ No

Opener's rebid of 3 of a new suit shows a singleton
or void and any strength.   ☐ Yes   ☐ No

Opener's rebid of 3 of a new suit
can include a singleton honor.   ☐ Yes   ☐ No

Opener's rebid of 3 of a new suit can include hands
with a strong 5-card side suit.   ☐ Yes   ☐ No

Opener's rebid of 4 of a new suit shows a 5-card suit
with 2 of the top 3 honors.   ☐ Yes   ☐ No

Opener's rebid of 4 of a new suit is only made
with fewer than 14 HCP.   ☐ Yes   ☐ No

Opener's rebid of 4 of a new suit denies a void.
                                       ☐ Yes   ☐ No

Opener's rebid of 4 of the trump suit shows
12-14 Bergen Points.   ☐ Yes   ☐ No

Opener's rebid of 3NT shows 15-17 Bergen Points.
                                       ☐ Yes   ☐ No

Opener's rebid of 3 of the trump suit shows
18+ Bergen Points.   ☐ Yes   ☐ No

Opener's rebid of 3 or 4 of the trump suit
or 3NT denies a short suit.   ☐ Yes   ☐ No

Opener's rebid of 4 of the trump suit
denies 3 aces.   ☐ Yes   ☐ No

Chapter 5
Splinter Bids

A Splinter Bid is a jump bid in a new suit that makes no sense as a natural bid. It shows a singleton or void in the suit bid, is forcing to game, and suggests the possibility of slam.

In my partnership with Larry Cohen, we treated all of the auctions in this chapter as Splinter Bids. Should you do the same? Probably not. One player's idea of a Splinter Bid might sound like a natural jump to his partner. **Without question, never make a Splinter Bid unless you're positive that your partner will understand your bid.**

Every partnership that uses Splinter Bids must do its homework. This volatile convention can't be treated lightly. You must discuss the convention and develop a partnership philosophy. Some possibilities are:

Level 1: The only Splinter Bids this group uses are double jumps in two basic situations:

*   By responder after an opening bid of 1♡ or 1♠;
*   By opener after a response of 1♡ or 1♠.

Level 2: In addition to double jumps, the partnership uses some single-jump Splinter Bids on the auctions listed in their notes, but that's all. Any jump made at the table is NOT a Splinter Bid if it's not in the notes.

Players who use Level 1 or Level 2 are very unlikely to have a misunderstanding.

Level 3: This group uses quite a few Splinter Bids, but have not had much discussion about them. They just assume that they'll be on the same wavelength.

Level 4: These partnerships also play quite a few Splinter Bids. Jump bids that make no sense as natural bids are splinters. However, they have discussed the subject at length, and have extensive notes. Larry Cohen and I used this approach.

Level 5: The freewheeling, "I never met a splinter I didn't like," approach. This group is totally enamored of Splinter Bids, and are eager to use them on auctions where other players would define the jump as a natural bid. They also use Splinter Bids at the five level.

Which approach best describes your partnership? I suggest that you circle one of the five choices.

Level 1   Level 2   Level 3   Level 4   Level 5

If your approach was not listed, then describe it here.

A great deal of discussion about how you play splinters can only help. Adding or deleting certain auctions from your Splinter Bid list is totally sensible. There is also nothing wrong with modifying, or even changing, your splinter philosophy at any time.

Partnership Checklist – Splinter Bids

Here is a series of Yes or No questions for you and your partner to answer together. When I feel strongly about the answer, I won't hesitate to make a recommendation.

Section A: Splinter Bid Essentials

1. It is okay to splinter with a singleton honor.

☐ Yes   ☐ No

I recommend: Yes
Because many teachers and authors have been so vocal in advising, "Don't splinter with a singleton king or ace," and because I feel so strongly that their advice is impractical, I must express the following:

Is splintering with a singleton honor perfect? No. Neither are most bids. A Splinter Bid tells your partner a great deal about your hand. That's good enough for me.

2. Other than a few logical exceptions, a Splinter Bid shows 4-card support for partner's suit.

☐ Yes   ☐ No

I recommend: Yes
Even if partner promised a 5-card suit, you should have 4+ trumps. If you splinter with only three trumps, you might not have enough trumps to ruff all of partner's losers. I will discuss the few logical exceptions later in this checklist.

3. When partner opens 1♡ or 1♠, a Splinter Bid promises 13-16 dummy points.

☐ Yes   ☐ No

Once again, I recommend: Yes

A Splinter Bid gives partner a specific description of your hand, and he becomes the boss. But if you actually have an ace more than what you promised, he will often make the wrong decision. With 17+ dummy points, I would respond Jacoby 2NT – imperfect, but practical and economical.

4. When partner opens 1♣ or 1♢, a double jump to three of a major is a Splinter Bid.

☐ Yes   ☐ No

5. A splinter promises controls in the other side suits.

☐ Yes   ☐ No

I recommend: No
You can't wait for perfect hands.

6. A Splinter Bid is forcing to game and suggests the possibility of slam.

☐ Yes   ☐ No

If you checked No, you probably use some variation of "mini-splinters." If so, I suggest you list them here.

Section B: Splinter Bids That Are Single Jumps

Below are a few of the many auctions where the player making the Splinter Bid jumps only one level. Each hand shown illustrates a Splinter Bid for that auction.

For auctions 7-9, it makes no difference if you are playing 1NT Forcing or 2/1 Game-Forcing.

For each of the following auctions, does your partnership treat the last bid as a splinter?

7.   1♡   1NT   ☐ Yes   ☐ No
            2♣   3♠

   ♠ 5   ♡ K 6   ◇ 8 7 5 4   ♣ A J 7 6 4 3

8.   1♣   1◇   ☐ Yes   ☐ No
            2♣   3♡

   ♠ A 8   ♡ 9   ◇ K Q 9 7 6 5   ♣ K 9 6 4

9.   1♡   2◇   ☐ Yes   ☐ No
            3♠

   ♠ —   ♡ A Q 8 6 3   ◇ K 7 5 4   ♣ A J 9 8

10.   1♠   2♡   ☐ Yes   ☐ No
            4♣

   ♠ A J 8 6 5 3   ♡ K Q 6 4   ◇ A 8   ♣ 8

11.   1♣   1♠   ☐ Yes   ☐ No
            2♡   4◇

   ♠ A K J 5 2   ♡ Q 8 6 4   ◇ 7   ♣ Q 8 5

12.　　　2♣　　　2◇　　　　☐ Yes　☐ No
　　　　　2♡　　　3♠

♠ 7　♡ J 8 6 3　◇ K 8 6 5 4　♣ 9 8 4

Because opener needs so much strength to open 2♣, responder does not need much strength to splinter.

Section C: More About Splinters

13. A Splinter Bid followed by a control-bid in that suit promises a void – not a singleton ace.

　　　☐ Yes　　　　　☐ No

As I said in chapter 3, I heartily recommend: Yes
When you have a fit, a void is a rare, but great, asset.
It can often result in magical slams without many HCP.
It is important to let partner know about your extreme good fortune. **As for a singleton ace, the worst location for any honor is in a short suit.**

14. Do we use delayed Splinter Bids?

　　　☐ Yes　　　　　☐ No

Consider this auction:

	Partner	*You*
	1♡	2♣
	2♡	4◇

Your jump to 4◇ must be a Splinter Bid because you would rebid 3◇ if you wanted to show a diamond suit. You didn't splinter at your first turn, so you don't have 4+ trumps. Your *delayed* jump to 4◇ told partner that you have only 3-card support.

After partner opens 1♡, the delayed splinter is a
sensible way to bid a hand such as:

♠ A Q 8 6   ♡ K 7 3   ◇ 2   ♣ K Q 8 7 4

The delayed splinter represents one of the logical
exceptions I mentioned when answering question #2:
"Does a Splinter Bid always show 4-card support for
partner's suit?"

15. After partner raises your suit, do we play
self-splinters?

☐ Yes   ☐ No

The other Splinter Bids that don't promise four cards
in partner's suit are called "self-splinters" becsause
the player making the Splinter Bid initiated the trump
suit himself.

Here is an example:

            1♣   1♠
            2♠   ???

    ♠ K 10 7 6 5 2   ♡ K 9 7   ◇ 3   ♣ A K 5

Slam is possible, but if partner has diamond values,
you wouldn't want to be in six. The best way to
express that is a 4◇ Splinter Bid. This bid tells
partner that you have slam interest with 0-1 diamonds.
He is then well-placed to evaluate slam prospects.

16. After a Transfer, do we play self-splinters?

　　　□ Yes　　　　　□ No

An opportunity for a self-splinter also occurs after a Jacoby Transfer. Suppose you hold the same hand as in #15.

　　♠ K 10 7 6 5 2　♡ K 9 7　◇ 3　♣ A K 5

This time, partner opens 1NT, you bid 2♡, and he bids the expected 2♠. You're interested in a spade slam, but your weak spade suit is a real concern. The best bid to show your hand is a 4◇ Splinter Bid.

17. After a 1NT response, is opener's jump reverse a self-splinter?

　　　□ Yes　　　　　□ No

Here is another chance for a self-splinter after a notrump bid. What should this jump show?

　　　　　1◇　　　　　　1NT
　　　　　3♡

A reverse of 2♡ would be forcing, so 3♡ should not show hearts. The jump reverse is a self-splinter, promising a very strong hand with 6+ cards in the suit opened and a singleton or void in the splinter suit. A hand such as:

　　♠ A 9 7　♡ 2　◇ A K Q 9 7 6　♣ A J 5

is one possibility. Depending on partner's hand, 3NT, 5♣, 5◇, 6♣, and 6◇ are all possible contracts.

18. Do you play Splinter Bids after opener bids a
major in response to Stayman?

☐ Yes   ☐ No

Here is another opportunity for a second-round
Splinter Bid after a 1NT opening bid:

	Partner	*You*
	1NT	2♣
	2♠	???

You hold:

♠ K J 8 2   ♡ 8   ◇ A Q 7 2   ♣ K J 7 3

You are very interested in a spade slam, but if partner
has heart strength, you would prefer to stop in game.
As long as partner definitely will understand your bid,
you should jump to 4♡. If there is a chance in the
world that partner *might* pass 4♡, find another bid.

19. My last potential Splinter Bid is definitely not "in."
But, because it is one that I have always played and
recommended, I can personally vouch for it.

1NT   2♣
2◇   ???

♠ K J 8 2   ♡ 8   ◇ A Q 7 2   ♣ K J 7 3

Unless answering 18 questions about Splinter Bids has
made you loopy, you'll recognize these cards as the
same ones you held in #18. Unfortunately, this time
partner's response to your 2♣ bid is not what you
wanted to hear. You would like to bid 3♡ as a splinter.
However, no one plays 3♡ as a Splinter Bid on this
auction, and I am NOT suggesting that you should.

Therefore, the normal bid at this point is 3NT, hoping that partner has heart strength.

Of course, you will go down in 3NT while cold for 6♣ if partner was dealt a hand such as:

♠ A 9 4   ♡ J 6 3   ♢ K J   ♣ A Q 10 4 2

Is that just an example of bad luck?

I would have some sympathy, but there is a sensible solution that is fun and not difficult. Define 1NT – 3♡ and 1NT – 3♠ as Splinter Bids. These responses are game-forcing, and show 9+ HCP and a singleton or void in the major. These hands do come up, and are far more important to show than the "in" responses where 3♡ and 3♠ show 5-5 in the majors.

Bidding Stayman with the 4-1-4-4 hand with 14 HCP worked out okay when partner bid spades – as long as you were able to follow with 4♡. But when partner bid 2♢, you were in terrible shape. You also would not have been thrilled if partner had bid 2♡. Although you would then bid 3NT with more confidence that partner had heart strength, because of your singleton there are many hands where you would belong in 6♣ or 6♢.

As is usually true when you have a singleton, the recommended strategy is to tell partner about it ASAP. If partner bids 3NT after 1NT – 3♡ (splinter), you could then pass with confidence.

Would you like to try 3♡ and 3♠ as Splinter Bids in response to 1NT?   ☐ Yes   ☐ No

Chapter 6
5NT Pick a Slam

In SBME, I gave the convention 5NT Pick a Slam my highest rating. I said, "Although it doesn't occur as often as other slam conventions, it is still my favorite." Why is that? Because *both players* are involved in the decision-making process, the partnership will arrive at the final contract only after mutual agreement.

Why is this convention necessary? Most of the time:

- Taking 12 tricks without a trump suit is *not* easy. It is much easier to take 12 tricks in a suit contract;

- Hands with a singleton play better in a suit contract;

- If you have the necessary strength and controls, 12 tricks are available in at least one of the suits – even if it is only a 7-card fit.

The convention works like this: When you know you belong in a small slam, but don't know where to play, a jump to 5NT asks partner for a suggestion.

After the 5NT Pick a Slam bid, partner can suggest a suit he is willing to play in. Possibilities include:

- Mentioning a new suit.

- Showing mild support for a suit you bid.

- Rebidding one of his suits with extra length or strength in that suit.

- Bidding 6NT if he has nothing worth mentioning or is *positive* that the hand belongs in notrump.

When playing 5NT Pick a Slam, you must remember:

- The 5NT bid is forcing;
- 5NT denies interest in a grand slam.

5NT Pick a Slam is unfamiliar to many players, so I will illustrate the convention with several examples.

1. *West*	*West*	*East*	*East*
♠ A K 10 6 5 3	2♣	2♦	♠ 4
♡ K	2♠	3♡	♡ A 10 8 7 4
♦ K Q	3♠	5NT	♦ A 9 6
♣ A K 10 9	6♣	Pass	♣ J 6 3 2

East was delighted to hear West open 2♣. However, his heart suit was not strong enough to respond 2♡, so he contented himself with a 2♦ waiting bid.

The auction proceeded naturally through West's 3♠ bid. East was then confronted with a crucial decision. Although his singleton spade was a liability, he did love his two aces. So, instead of bidding 3NT, he made the decision to play in slam.

Too many players who reached the same conclusion would have bid an inappropriate 4NT or an aimless 6NT. However, East was careful to bid a flexible 5NT, which asked partner to express his opinion. West did have a suit he was happy to mention, and that suited East just fine.

6♣ was easy – making six. When spades split 4-2, 6♠ and 6NT would also have been easy – down one.

2. West	West	East	East
♠ 8	1♥	1♠	♠ A Q 7 6 5 2
♥ A K 8 6 3	3◇	3♠	♥ 7
◇ K Q J 10	3NT	5NT	◇ A 9 2
♣ K Q J	6◇	Pass	♣ A 9 4

Once West promised 19+ points with his jump-shift, East knew that the partnership had enough strength for slam. The only question to resolve was which strain (suit or notrump) to play in.

The first five bids were easy. After 3NT, most players would have jumped to 6NT. As you can see, because of the misfit, 6NT is an awful contract. Although E-W have 33 HCP, West needs the spade finesse plus a 3-3 spade split. That is an 18% slam. No thanks.

Fortunately, this East was made of sterner stuff. There was no rush to bid 6NT. Instead, he made the careful, "let's see what partner has to say," 5NT bid.

West knew that his singleton in East's long suit would be a liability in notrump. West didn't have extra length in either of his two suits, but he did have exquisite diamonds. Therefore he bid 6◇. Whether West had five diamonds or a quality 4-card suit, a diamond slam sounded good to East.

East's singleton heart was an asset in a suit contract, so 6◇ was a great contract. In fact, with normal splits, 7◇ will make. So much for, "We've got 33 HCP, so bid 6NT now and think later."

3. *West*	*West*	*East*	*East*
♠ K Q	1NT	2♣	♠ A 6 5 3
♡ A Q	2◇	3♡	♡ K J 10 8 6
◇ K 7 4 2	3NT	5NT	◇ A 8 5
♣ Q 9 6 5 2	6♡	Pass	♣ A

To avoid a rebid problem, West opened 1NT despite the two doubletons. I totally agree, and advise doing so with many similar hands. After West's 2◇ bid, East's jump to 3♡ was forcing and unlimited. Because East was still interested in hearts after West denied a 4-card major, East promised 5+ cards in the suit. Of course, if East did not have spades, he would have transferred rather than bidding Stayman. Therefore, his 3♡ bid also promised four spades. With only two hearts, West retreated to 3NT.

East's hand was worth 19 *starting points*. 16 HCP + 1 for Adjust-3 (4 upgrades, 1 downgrade) + 1 (quality heart suit) + 1 (5-card suit) = 19.

Once West opened 1NT, East was never stopping short of slam. But there was no rush to bid 6NT. Instead, he bid 5NT Pick a Slam.

If West's clubs were stronger, he would have bid 6♣ to suggest playing slam in that suit. West's 3NT bid had denied three hearts, so he sensibly supported hearts with his ♡AQ. East was happy to hear it.

Because West could ruff a spade, 6♡ was easy. After a club lead, 6NT was hopeless. But, as is often the case, 6NT didn't rate to make on any lead.

Here are three more examples of 5NT Pick a Slam in action. West has a different hand for each example, but the East cards are unchanged. On all three hands, West opens 1NT and East: transfers to hearts, shows diamonds, and then bids 5NT Pick a Slam.

4. *West*	*West*	*East*	*East*
♠ K Q 9 8	1NT	2◇	♠ A
♡ K 2	2♡	3◇	♡ Q 7 5 4 3
◇ K Q 5	3NT	5NT	◇ A J 9 2
♣ K J 9 2	6NT	Pass	♣ A Q 4

With 17 HCP and strength in the unbid suits, West is *eager* to bid 6NT.

5. *West*	*West*	*East*	*East*
♠ Q J 2	1NT	2◇	♠ A
♡ K 10	2♡	3◇	♡ Q 7 5 4 3
◇ K Q 5	3NT	5NT	◇ A J 9 2
♣ K J 10 9 3	6♣	Pass	♣ A Q 4

With 15 HCP, nice clubs, and shaky spades, West is *eager* to bid 6♣ to show his long suit. With strong 3-card support, East is happy to pass.

6. *West*	*West*	*East*	*East*
♠ K Q J 2	1NT	2◇	♠ A
♡ K 6 2	2♡	3◇	♡ Q 7 5 4 3
◇ K Q 3	3♡	5NT	◇ A J 9 2
♣ K 3 2	6NT	Pass	♣ A Q 4

With his weak suit, East is *not eager* to settle for hearts when West bid 3♡. With 17 HCP, a flat hand, and only moderate hearts, West is happy to bid 6NT.

When discussing this convention in SBME, I defined the setting as Swiss Teams. I did this intentionally, so readers would not be thinking about getting a better matchpoint score if they could bid and make 6NT.

Do I recommend 5NT Pick a Slam for team play only? Nothing could be further from the truth. Regardless of the form of scoring, taking 12 tricks without a trump suit is rarely easy. Doing so on a misfit often borders on the impossible.

Partnership Checklist – 5NT Pick a Slam

For all statements below, I recommend: Yes

1. We use 5NT Pick a Slam for both matchpoints and team games. ☐ Yes ☐ No

2. A jump to 5NT is always forcing. ☐ Yes ☐ No

3. 5NT denies interest in a grand slam.
    ☐ Yes ☐ No

4. 6NT is not your favorite slam.
    ☐ Yes ☐ No

5. We are willing to play slam in a strong 7-card trump fit. ☐ Yes ☐ No

6. A jump to 5NT is not the Grand Slam Force. ☐ Yes ☐ No

7. A jump to 5NT is never quantitative.
    ☐ Yes ☐ No

Chapter 7
Blackwood and RKC

A note about this chapter: The first half is directed to all players – regardless of how you respond to 4NT. The second half concentrates on RKC. Although most RKC players prefer 1430, my RKC discussion applies equally well to players and partnerships who prefer playing 3014.

Blackwood

Defintely the world's most popular convention – and the most over-used. This is true regardless of what type of responses you use. Therefore, the following (in no special order) are my Top 10 recommendations to help you avoid over-using Blackwood.

1. Use control-bidding more often. It is definitely more efficient than Blackwood. Why is that?

- It involves both players;

- You learn the location of partner's controls;

- You can stop in game if you choose to;

- You still have a chance to use Blackwood.

For those players who are reluctant to use control bids, Italian control-bidding is not difficult – it just takes some getting used to. If you give it a try, I bet you'll agree that it is both more fun to play and more efficient to use than, "We can't wait to bid 4NT."

2. If you know what slam you want to play in, don't bother bidding 4NT. I can't tell you how many times I've seen the following: A player knows that his side has 33+ total points, enough aces (or keycards) for slam, and no interest in a grand slam. What happens next? He bids 4NT, gets the expected irrelevant response, and bids a small slam. Meanwhile, the opponents have had a chance to exchange information about their hands by making (or failing to make) a lead-directing double.

There is no law that says you must bid 4NT on every slam hand. Keep in mind: "He who knows, goes."

3. When the agreed trump suit is not spades, using Blackwood without many aces (or keycards) can easily get you too high. Instead, prefer to use a control-bid.

4. Don't close your eyes and bid 4NT just because you fell in love with a very strong hand and hoped to get lucky.

5. If you don't have controls in all the unbid suits, avoid using Blackwood unless you're sure you belong in slam and have no alternative.

6. When partner opens one of a suit, it is rarely correct to respond 4NT at your first turn. Go slowly with good hands to obtain as much useful information as possible about partner's hand.

7. Because Blackwood is not a two-way street, avoid bidding 4NT if you are not in a position to decide the fate of the partnership on your own.

8. If you're not sure if your side has 33+ total points, don't use Blackwood. Partner's response will NOT tell you if he has extra values. Instead, prefer to make a bid that invites partner to let you know how *he* feels about his hand.

9. Be wary of misfits. Taking 12 tricks when both players dislike each other's suits can be a nightmare, even if your side has a lot of "points." However, if you are confident that your side belongs in slam, but have not found a good fit, don't bid 4NT or jump to 6NT.

Instead, on these situations it is usually correct to bid 5NT Pick a Slam. This very useful convention will often uncover a playable trump suit that will allow you to take 12 tricks by ruffing some of your losers. There are many hands where 6NT has no play – but slam is makable in a chunky 7-card fit. You have nothing to lose by bidding 5NT. If you are not able to find a worthwhile trump suit, you can then settle for the same 6NT contract that you were heading for.

10. On some auctions, 4NT is NOT Blackwood. This is especially true when notrump has been bid earlier. If you are not sure how partner will interpret 4NT, find another bid.

After my 3-page diatribe of suggestions why you *should not* be eager to use Blackwood, can I say anything positive about the convention? Absolutely.

Blackwood Encouragement

Although I know experts who have nothing good to say about Blackwood, I don't feel that way. You will see many hands in my books where I recommend bidding 4NT – at the appropriate time. The thrust of my previous three pages was NOT to suggest that you give up Blackwood; but instead, to consider alternatives, rather than simply relying on 4NT as an all-purpose, cure for all ills, "can't live without it" crutch.

When your side has 33+ total points, controls in all of the side suits, and you know what to do over any response, using Blackwood to find out about aces (or keycards) is an excellent idea.

Too many players believe there is something very wrong with the weaker hand bidding Blackwood. This is definitely not true. The previous paragraph makes it clear that the player who should bid 4NT is the one who *knows* that the partnership belongs in slam. It says nothing about which player has the majority of the HCP.

Because Italian control-bidding treats second-round controls the same as first-round controls, following up a control-bidding auction with Blackwood is an absolute necessity. The conventions complement each other nicely and constitute a dynamic 1-2 punch.

Partnership Checklist – Blackwood

Whether you use traditional responses or RKC, answer Yes or No for the following questions.

1. If partner bids 4NT, then 5NT, is he inviting you to bid seven?

☐ Yes   ☐ No

I recommend: Yes
If partner wants to play in six, he didn't need to bid 5NT. So, if you have a source of tricks or are sure you have the right hand for seven – it's okay to bid it.

2. In SBME, this is what I suggested for responding to 4NT when you have a void:

The phrases "0 or 2" and "1 or 3" refer to:
the number of aces for ace-askers; or
the number of keycards for RKC pairs.

5NT = 0 or 2, and a void.
6 in a new suit shows 1 or 3, and a void in the suit.
6 of the trump suit shows 1 or 3, and a void in a suit that is higher-ranking than your trump suit.

Do you agree with the above?

☐ Yes   ☐ No

If No, describe your agreements below.

RKC: Handle With Care

In SBME I said: "Whether you play 1430 or 3014, this convention is fraught with danger." That does not mean that it has no merit. I am definitely NOT advocating that RKC players stop playing RKC. What do I recommend? If a suit was bid and raised, respond RKC. If not, use traditional responses.

Partnership Checklist – RKC

Here are some more questions for your partnership. Check the appropriate box for each question.

Question 1: Which RKC response do we use?

☐ 1430   ☐ 3014

My recommendation: play the one that YOU prefer. Most RKC players these days swear by 1430. Some advanced players vary their responses based on the type of auction! That has as much appeal to me as walking barefoot on hot coals.

Question 2: Do we use any conventions that ask for aces or keycards besides RKC and Gerber?

☐ Yes   ☐ No

If you answered Yes, describe your agreements below in detail. Some possibilities here are: Kickback, Exclusion, and Redwood.

Question 3: When there is no agreed trump suit, do we play that the last-bid suit is "trumps" for showing keycards?

☐ Yes   ☐ No

When I ask this question, the inevitable response is an enthusiastic "Yes." As a non-admirer of *last-bid suit*, I was amused when my surveys indicated uncertainty amongst the ranks on certain auctions. Regardless, do indicate your agreement on this important issue.

Question 4: Are there any auctions where we use traditional responses to 4NT? If Yes, which ones?

☐ Yes   ☐ No

You already know my thoughts when no suit has been bid and raised. Eddie Kantar, who invented 1430, suggests: "RKC responses should not be used unless a trump suit was clearly indicated." Many experts advocate: "After a response of 4NT to an opening bid in a suit, use traditional Blackwood – not RKC." Use the space below to indicate your agreements.

Question 5: When a player responds 5♡ or 5♠, he might have 5 keycards, rather than 2.

☐ Yes   ☐ No

Although it is rare, I recommend: Yes
Bidding 4NT with zero keycards does happen.

Question 6. Do we use all, some, or none of the "queen ask?"

This occurs when: You bid 4NT, partner responds 5♣ or 5♢, you are missing the trump queen, and your side has fewer than 10 trumps.

☐ All   ☐ Some   ☐ None

I recommend: each pair does what makes them happy.

Question 7. When partner bids 4NT and then follows with 5NT, how do you respond?

☐   Traditional – number of kings in side suits.

☐   Control-bid the cheapest king, but only when spades are trumps. Some pairs have additional agreements here to learn about other kings as well.

☐   Control-bid the cheapest king regardless of which suit is trumps.

The third approach does have an upside, but is accident-prone. Which approach should you use? It's your choice; but as I learned long ago, I much prefer KISSing to being tortured.

Question 8. When responding to 4NT with 2 keycards, if you know your side has 10+ trumps, do you bid 5♠ without the queen of trumps?

☐ Yes   ☐ No

I recommend: Yes
With 10+ trumps, you don't expect to lose a trick to an opponent's trump queen. Also, if partner has the trump queen, he will know about your extra trump. That could be all he needs to bid seven.

Question 9. When partner responds 5♣ or 5♢ to 4NT, if you sign off in five of the agreed suit, will he bid on with the higher number of keycards?
Please circle the appropriate answer.

No   Our agreement is: the 4NT bidder is the boss.

Yes   He must, that is our agreement.

Maybe   Our agreements vary based on the auction.

???   We have no agreement.

Why the big deal? If the 4NT bidder hesitates before signing off, he has conveyed unauthorized information. This recurring problem is referred to as "Hesitation Blackwood" and can cause a *big mess.* The solution is: *before* bidding 4NT, decide what you plan to bid if partner responds 5♣ or 5♢. A sign-off will then be in tempo, so whether partner bids or passes, there won't be a Hesitation Blackwood problem. I suggest having your written agreements with you; that way, you can prove that partner's action was based on your system.

(answers are on next page)

Partner opens 1♡.

First, count your *starting points* (page 12).

Then, count your dummy points (page 14).

What bid would you make?

1. ♠ A 8 6 5 3   ♡ K 10 4   ◇ A K 6 4   ♣ 3

starting points:

dummy points:

What's your bid?

2. ♠ A Q 5   ♡ K J 6 2   ◇ 4   ♣ A 10 7 5 3

starting points:

dummy points:

What's your bid?

3. ♠ K 10 7 6 4   ♡ A 10 8 6   ◇ 4   ♣ K J 3

starting points:

dummy points:

What's your bid?

Answers

Partner opens 1♡.

1.   ♠ A 8 6 5 3   ♡ K 10 4   ◇ A K 6 4   ♣ 3
14 HCP.
Adjust-3: Add 1 point (3 upgrades, no downgrades).
Length points: Add 1 point (5-card spade suit).
16 *starting points* (14 + 1 + 1 = 16).
Short suits: Add 2 points (singleton with 3 trumps).
Total: 18 dummy points (16 + 2 = 18).
Bid 1♠. You have a heart fit and expect to become the
dummy in a heart contract. But you should not bid
2NT nor make a Splinter Bid with only a 3-card fit.

2.   ♠ A Q 5   ♡ K J 6 2   ◇ 4   ♣ A 10 7 5 3
14 HCP.
Adjust-3: No adjustment (3 upgrades, 2 downgrades).
Length: Add 1 point (5-card club suit).
15 *starting points* (14 + 1 = 15).
15 + 3 (singleton with 4 trumps) = 18 dummy points.
Bid 2NT. This hand is too strong to splinter, and
showing clubs is not important. Support with support.

3.   ♠ K 10 7 6 4   ♡ A 10 8 6   ◇ 4   ♣ K J 3
11 HCP.
Adjust-3: No adjustment (3 upgrades, 1 downgrade).
Length: Add 1 point (5-card spade suit).
12 *starting points* (11 + 1 = 12).
12 + 3 (singleton with 4 trumps) = 15 dummy points.
Bid 4◇. A textbook example of a Splinter Bid.
After describing your hand in one bid, partner should
be well-placed to evaluate slam chances.

West	*West*	*East*	*East*
♠ K J 8 7 4	1♠	2NT	♠ A 9 6 5 3
♡ K 10 4	3♣	3◇	♡ A Q
◇ A J 6 4 3	3♡	3♠	◇ K 8 2
♣ —	4♣	4NT	♣ Q J 4
	5♡	7♠	

West:

12 HCP + 2 (two 5-card suits) = 14 starting points.
14 + 4 (void) + 1 (side suit) = 19 Bergen Points.

East:

16 HCP + 1 (5-card suit) = 17 starting points.
17 + 1 (doubleton) = 18 dummy points.

Bidding seven is never easy, but I think this one is logical.   Here's a summary of what the bids showed.

3♣:   Singleton or void in clubs
3◇:   Control-bid
3♡:   Control-bid
3♠:   Waiting bid. Voids are rare, but they are magical.
        When partner shows a short suit, give him a chance to show a void.
4♣:   Club void
4NT: 1430
5♡:   2 keycards. Denied extra length in trumps.
7♠:   At this point, West had promised five spades headed by the king, a club void, the heart king, and the diamond ace. Therefore, East could see that his side had no losers, so he bid 7♠.

Highly Recommended

See page 64 for ordering information

Hardcover Books by Marty Bergen

Slam Bidding Made Easier – How to Bid Good Slams	$24.95
Declarer Play the Bergen Way – 2005 Book of the Year	$18.95
POINTS SCHMOINTS! –All-Time Bestseller	$19.95
More POINTS SCHMOINTS!	$19.95
More Declarer Play the Bergen Way	$18.95
Bergen for the Defense	$18.95
MARTY SEZ... Volume 1	$17.95
MARTY SEZ... Volume 2	$17.95
MARTY SEZ... Volume 3	$17.95

•• VERY SPECIAL OFFER ••

Buy one of these hardcover books from Marty
and receive a **free** copy of any of his nine softcover books.
Buy 2 hardcovers and get 3 free softcover books!
Buy 3 hardcovers and get 5 free softcover books!
Personalized autographs available upon request.
In addition, each order of *Slam Bidding Made Easier*
will be accompanied by a free copy
of Marty's brand-new workbook:
Better Slam Bidding with Bergen

Softcover Books by Marty Bergen
Buy 2, then get 1 (equal or lesser price) FREE!

Bergen's Best Bridge Tips	$7.95
Bergen's Best Bridge Quizzes, Vol. 1	$7.95
To Open or Not to Open	$6.95
Better Rebidding with Bergen	$7.95
Understanding 1NT Forcing	$5.95
Hand Evaluation: Points, Schmoints!	$7.95
Introduction to Negative Doubles	$8.95
Negative Doubles	$10.95
Better Slam Bidding with Bergen	$9.95

Bridge Cruises with Marty Bergen

To be on the mailing list for Marty's cruises,
call Bruce Travel at 1-800-367-9980.
To participate in bridge activities,
you must book the cruise with Bruce Travel.

All Bergen Cruises Feature:

**Marty's daily lessons with brand-new material;
free drawing to play duplicate with Marty;
free private lesson for 5+ signing up together;
free Bergen book for early sign up;
plenty of bridge (ACBL masterpoints).**

An Excellent Book for Slam Bidding Practice

Larry Cohen's Bidding Challenge $15.95
192 pages. Read Larry's analysis of many slam hands.
Buy Larry's book and get Marty's workbook FREE!

Interactive CDs

FREE SHIPPING (in the U.S.) if you mention this book

by Marty Bergen
    POINTS SCHMOINTS!   ~~$29.95~~ $25
    Marty Sez....   ~~$24.95~~ $20
Very Special Offer: Get both Bergen CDs for $30!
For free demos, e-mail Marty at: mbergen@mindspring.com

    4 CDs by Larry Cohen   ~~$29.95~~ $19 each
Free demos available at: http://www.larryco.com/index.html

    2 CDs by Kit Woolsey   ~~$29.95~~ $19 each

Software By Fred Gitelman
"Best software ever created for improving declarer play."
    Bridge Master 2000   ~~$59.95~~ $48

**Mention this book and receive a free Bergen softcover
(choice of 7) with each Gitelman CD.**

Excellent Bridge Websites
(each site is free)

www.larryco.com   Vist Larry Cohen's site for lots of bridge articles, features and instruction.

www.carlritner.com   Great deals on used bridge books. An amazing inventory of out-of-print books. Many of the books were sent from the ACBL Library.

www.bridgeguys.com   A wealth of information, including an extensive glossary. If you need info, request it – and they will deliver.

www.bridgebase.com   Bridge Base Online (BBO). A free site where you can play. Just click on the link: "Click here to play or watch bridge." BBO offers: duplicate bridge, team matches, rubber bridge, and tournaments that award prize money or masterpoints. BBO also provides facilities to improve your game, and live broadcasts of major events with expert analysis.

ORDERING INFORMATION

To place your order, call Marty toll-free at:
1-800-386-7432
or email him at mbergen@mindspring.com
Major credit cards are welcome (not AMEX)
Or send a check or money order (U.S. funds), to:
Marty Bergen
9 River Chase Terrace
Palm Beach Gardens, FL 33418-6817
If ordering by mail, call or email for S&H details.